PERPETUAL PEACE

PERPETUAL PEACE

IMMANUEL KANT

COSIMO CLASSICS
NEW YORK

Library of Congress Cataloging-in-Publication Data
A catalog record for this book is available from the Library of Congress

Cover design by www.wiselephant.com

ISBN: 1-59605-549-9

CONTENTS

FIRST SECTION : *Containing the Preliminary Articles of Perpetual Peace Between States*   3

SECOND SECTION : *Containing the Definitive Articles of a Perpetual Peace Between States*   9

FIRST SUPPLEMENT : *Concerning the Guarantee of Perpetual Peace*   20

SECOND SUPPLEMENT : *A Secret Article for Perpetual Peace*   28

APPENDIX I : *On the Disagreement Between Morals and Politics with Reference to Perpetual Peace*   31

APPENDIX II : *Concerning the Harmony of Politics with Morals According to the Transcendental Idea of Public Right*   45

NOTES   55

FIRST SECTION

1. *No treaty of peace shall be regarded as valid if made with the secret reservation of material for a future war.*

For then it would be a mere truce, a mere suspension of hostilities, not peace. A peace signifies the end of all hostilities and to attach to it the epithet "eternal" is not only a verbal pleonasm, but matter of suspicion. The causes of a future war existing, although perhaps not yet known to the high contracting parties themselves, are entirely annihilated by the conclusion of peace, however acutely they may be ferreted out of documents in the public archives. There may be a mental reservation of old claims to be thought out at a future time, which are, none of them, mentioned at this stage because both parties are too much exhausted to continue the war, while the evil intention remains of using the first favorable opportunity for further hostilities. Diplomacy of this kind only Jesuitical casuistry can justify: it is beneath the dignity of a ruler, just as acquiescence in such processes of reasoning is beneath the dignity of his minister, if one judges the facts as they really are.

If, however, according to present enlightened ideas of political wisdom, the true glory of a state lies in the uninterrupted development of its power by every possible means, this judgment must certainly strike one as scholastic and pedantic.

3

2. *No state having an independent existence—whether it be great or small—shall be acquired by another through inheritance, exchange, purchase or donation.*

For a state is not a property (*patrimonium*), as may be the ground on which its people are settled. It is a society of human beings over whom no one but itself has the right to rule and to dispose. Like the trunk of a tree, it has its own roots, and to graft it on to another state is to do away with its existence as a moral person, and to make of it a thing. Hence it is in contradiction to the idea of the original contract without which no right over a people is thinkable.[1]* Everyone knows to what danger the bias in favor of these modes of acquisition has brought Europe (in other parts of the world it has never been known). The custom of marriage between states, as if they were individuals, has survived even up to the most recent times, and is regarded partly as a new kind of industry by which ascendancy may be acquired through family alliances, without any expenditure of strength; partly as a device for territorial expansion. Moreover, the hiring out of the troops of one state to another to fight against an enemy not at war with their native country is to be reckoned in this connection; for the subjects are in this way used and abused at will as personal property.

3. *Standing armies shall be abolished in course of time.*

For they are always threatening other states with war by appearing to be in constant readiness to fight. They incite the various states to outrival one another in the number of their soldiers, and to this number no limit can be set. Now, since owing to the sums devoted to this purpose, peace at last becomes even more oppressive than a short war, these

* Numerals refer to Kant's notes on pages 55–65.

standing armies are themselves the cause of wars of aggression, undertaken in order to get rid of this burden. To which we must add the practice of hiring men to kill or to be killed seems to imply a use of them as mere machines and instruments in the hand of another (namely, the state) which cannot easily be reconciled with the right of humanity in our own person. The matter stands quite differently in the case of voluntary periodical military exercise on the part of citizens of the state, who thereby seek to secure themselves and their country against attack from without.

The accumulation of treasure in a state would in the same way be regarded by other states as a menace of war, and might compel them to anticipate this by striking the first blow. For of the three forces, the power of arms, the power of alliance, and the power of money, the last might well become the most reliable instrument of war did not the difficulty of ascertaining the amount stand in the way.

4. *No national debts shall be contracted in connection with the external affairs of the state.*

This source of help is above suspicion where assistance is sought outside or within the state, on behalf of the economic administration of the country (for instance, the improvements of the roads, the settlement and support of new colonies, the establishment of granaries to provide against seasons of scarcity, and so on). But, as a common weapon used by the Powers against one another, a credit system under which debts go on indefinitely increasing and are yet always assured against immediate claims (because all the creditors do not put in their claim at once) is a dangerous money power. This ingenious invention of a commercial people in the present century is, in other words, a treasure for the carrying on of war which may exceed the treasures of all the other states taken together, and can only be exhausted by a threatening deficiency in the taxes—an event, however, which will long be kept off by the very briskness of commerce resulting from the reaction of this system on industry and trade. The ease, then, with which war may be waged, coupled with the inclination of rulers towards it— an inclination which seems to be implanted in human nature —is a great obstacle in the way of perpetual peace. The prohibition of this system must be laid down as a preliminary article of perpetual peace, all the more necessarily because the final inevitable bankruptcy of the state in question must involve in the loss many who are innocent, and this would be a public injury to these states. Therefore other nations are at least justified in uniting themselves against such an one and its pretensions.

5. *No state shall violently interfere with the constitution and administration of another.*

For what can justify it in so doing? The scandal which is here presented to the subjects of another state? The erring state can much more serve as a warning by exemplifying the great evils which a nation draws down on itself through its own lawlessness. Moreover, the bad example which one free person gives another (as *scandalum acceptum*) does no injury to the latter. In this connection, it is true, we cannot count the case of a state which has become split up through internal corruption into two parts, each of them representing by itself an individual state which lays claim to the whole. Here the yielding of assistance to one faction could not be reckoned as interference on the part of a foreign state with the constitution of another, for here anarchy prevails. So long, however, as the inner strife has not yet reached this stage the interference of other powers would be a violation of the rights of an independent nation which is only struggling with internal disease. It would therefore itself cause a scandal, and make the autonomy of all states insecure.

6. *No state at war with another shall countenance such modes of hostility as would make mutual confidence impossible in a subsequent state of peace: such are the employment of assassins or of poisoners, the violation of articles of surrender, and the instigation of treason in the hostile state.*

These are dishonorable stratagems. For some kind of confidence in the disposition of the enemy must exist even in the midst of war, as otherwise peace could not be concluded, and the hostilities would pass into a war of extermination. War, however, is only our wretched expedient of asserting a right by force—an expedient adopted in the state of nature, where no court of justice exists which could settle the matter in dispute. In circumstances like these, neither of the two parties can be called an unjust enemy because this form of speech presupposes a legal decision: the issue of the conflict—just as in the case of the so-called judgments of God—decides on which side right is. Between states, however, no punitive war is thinkable because between them a relation of superior and inferior does not exist. Whence it follows that a war of extermination, where the process of annihilation would strike both parties at once and all right as well, would bring about perpetual peace only in the great graveyard of the human race. Such a war, then, and therefore also the use of all means which lead to it, must be absolutely forbidden. That the methods just mentioned do inevitably lead to this result is obvious from the fact that these infernal arts, already vile in themselves, on coming into use, are not long confined to the sphere of war. Take, for example, the use of spies. Here only the dishonesty of others is made use of; but vices such as these, when once encouraged, cannot in the nature of things be stamped out and would be carried over into the state of peace, where their presence would be utterly destructive to the purpose of that state.

Although the laws stated are, objectively regarded (i.e. in so far as they affect the action of rulers), purely prohibitive laws (*leges prohibitivae*), some of them (*leges strictae*) are strictly valid without regard to circumstances and urgently require to be enforced. Such are Articles 1, 5, and 6. Others, again—like Articles 2, 3, and 4—although not indeed exceptions to the maxims of law, yet in respect of the practical application of these maxims, allow subjectively of a certain latitude to suit particular circumstances. The enforcement of these *leges latae* may be legitimately put off, so long as we do not lose sight of the ends at which they aim. This purpose of reform does not permit of the deferment of an act of restitution (as, for example, the restoration to certain states of freedom of which they have been deprived in the manner described in Article 2) to an infinitely distant date—as Augustus used to say, to the "Greek Kalends," a day that will never come. This would be to sanction non-restitution. Delay is permitted only with the intention that restitution should not be made too precipitately and so defeat the purpose we have in view. For the prohibition refers here only to the *mode of acquisition* which is to be no longer valid, and not to the *fact of possession* which, although indeed it has not the necessary title of right, yet at the time of so-called acquisition was held legal by all states, in accordance with the public opinion of the time.[2]

SECOND SECTION

Containing the Definitive Articles of a Perpetual Peace Between States

A STATE of peace among men who live side by side is not the natural state (*status naturalis*), which is rather to be described as a state of war: that is to say, although there is not perhaps always actual open hostility, yet there is a constant threatening that an outbreak may occur. Thus the state of peace must be *established*. For the mere cessation of hostilities is no guarantee of continued peaceful relations, and unless this guarantee is given by every individual to his neighbor—which can only be done in a state of society regulated by law—one man is at liberty to challenge another and treat him as an enemy.[3]

FIRST DEFINITIVE ARTICLE OF PERPETUAL PEACE

I. *The civil constitution of each state shall be republican.*
The only constitution which has its origin in the idea of the original contract, upon which the lawful legislation of every nation must be based, is the republican.[4] It is a constitution, in the first place, founded in accordance with the principle of the freedom of the members of society as human beings; secondly, in accordance with the principle of the dependence of all, as subjects, on a common legislation; and, thirdly, in accordance with the law of the equality of the members as citizens. It is then, looking at the question of right, the only constitution whose fundamental principles lie at the basis of every form of civil constitution. And the

only question for us now is whether it is also the one constitution which can lead to perpetual peace.

Now the republican constitution, apart from the soundness of its origin, since it arose from the pure source of the concept of right, has also the prospect of attaining the desired result—namely, perpetual peace. And the reason is this. If, as must be so under this constitution, the consent of the subjects is required to determine whether there shall be war or not, nothing is more natural than that they should weigh the matter well, before undertaking such a bad business. For in decreeing war, they would, of necessity, be resolving to bring down the miseries of war upon their country. This implies: they must fight themselves; they must hand over the costs of the war out of their own property; they must do their poor best to make good the devastation which it leaves behind; and finally, as a crowning ill, they have to accept a burden of debt which will embitter even peace itself, and which they can never pay off on account of the new wars which are always impending. On the other hand, in a government where the subject is not a citizen holding a vote (i.e. in a constitution which is not republican), the plunging into war is the least serious thing in the world. For the ruler is not a citizen but the owner of the state, and does not lose a whit by the war, while he goes on enjoying the delights of his table or sport, or of his pleasure palaces and gala days. He can therefore decide on war for the most trifling reasons, as if it were a kind of pleasure party. Any justification of it that is necessary for the sake of decency he can leave without concern to the diplomatic corps who are always only too ready with their services.

The following remarks must be made in order that we may not fall into the common error of confusing the republican with the democratic constitution. The forms of the state (*civitas*) may be classified according to either of two principles of division: the difference of the persons who hold the supreme authority in the state, and the manner in which the people are governed by their ruler, whoever he may be. The first is properly called the form of sovereignty (*forma imperii*), and there can be only three constitutions differing in this respect: where, namely, the supreme authority belongs to only one, to several individuals working together, or to the whole people constituting the civil society. Thus we have autocracy or the sovereignty of a monarch, aristocracy or the sovereignty of the nobility, and democracy or the sovereignty of the people.

The second principle of division is the form of government (*forma regiminis*), and refers to the way in which the state makes use of its supreme power: for the manner of government is based on the constitution, itself the act of that universal will which transforms a multitude into a nation. In this respect the form of government is either republican or despotic. Republicanism is the political principle of severing the executive power of the government from the legislature. Despotism is that principle in pursuance of which the state arbitrarily puts into effect laws which it has itself made: consequently it is the administration of the public will, but this is identical with the private will of the ruler. Of these three forms of a state, democracy, in the proper sense of the word, is of necessity despotism, because it establishes an executive power, since all decree regarding —and, if need be, against—any individual who dissents from them. Therefore, the "whole people," so-called, who carry their measure are really not all, but only a majority: so that here the universal will is in contradiction with itself and with the principle of freedom.

Every form of government, in fact, which is not representative is really no true constitution at all, because a lawgiver may no more be, in one and the same person, the ad-

ministrator of his own will than the universal major premise
of a syllogism may be, at the same time, the subsumption
under itself of the particulars contained in the minor premise. And, although the other two constitutions—autocracy
and aristocracy—are always defective in so far as they leave
the way open for such a form of government, yet there is at
least always a possibility in these cases that they may take
the form of a government in accordance with the spirit of
a representative system. Thus Frederick the Great used at
least to *say* that he was "merely the highest servant[5] of the
state." The democratic constitution, on the other hand,
makes this impossible, because under such a government
everyone wishes to be master. We may therefore say that the
smaller the staff of the executive—that is to say, the number
of rulers—and the more real, on the other hand, their representation of the people, so much the more is the government of the state in accordance with a possible republicanism; and it may hope, by gradual reforms, to raise itself
to that standard. For this reason, it is more difficult under
an aristocracy than under a monarchy—while under a
democracy it is impossible except by a violent revolution—
to attain to this, the one perfectly lawful constitution. The
kind of government,[6] however, is of infinitely more im-
portance to the people than the kind of constitution, although the greater or less aptitude of a people for this ideal
greatly depends upon such external form. The form of government, however, if it is to be in accordance with the idea
of right, must embody the representative system in which
alone a republican form of administration is possible, and
without which it is despotic and violent—be the constitution what it may. None of the ancient so-called republics
were aware of this, and they necessarily slipped into absolute despotism which, of all despotisms, is most endurable
under the sovereignty of one individual.

SECOND DEFINITIVE ARTICLE OF PERPETUAL PEACE

II. *The law of nations shall be founded on a federation of free states.*

Nations, as states, may be judged like individuals who, living in the natural state of society—that is to say, uncontrolled by external law—injure one another through their very proximity. Every state, for the sake of its own security, may—and ought to—demand that its neighbor should submit itself to conditions similar to those of the civil society where the right of every individual is guaranteed. This would give rise to a federation of nations, which, however, would not have to be a State of nations. That would involve a contradiction. For the term "state" implies the relation of one who rules to those who obey—that is to say, of lawgiver to the subject people: and many nations in one state would constitute only one nation, which contradicts our hypothesis, since here we have to consider the right of one nation against another, in so far as they are so many separate states and are not to be fused into one.

The attachment of savages to their lawless liberty, the fact that they would rather be at hopeless variance with one another than submit themselves to a legal authority constituted by themselves, that they therefore prefer their senseless freedom to a reason-governed liberty, is regarded by us with profound contempt as barbarism and uncivilization and the brutal degradation of humanity. So one would think that civilized races, each formed into a state by itself, must come out of such an abandoned condition as soon as they possibly can. On the contrary, however, every state thinks rather that its majesty (the "majesty" of a people is an absurd expression) lies just in the very fact that it is subject to no external legal authority; and the glory of the ruler consists in this, that, without his requiring to expose himself to danger, thousands stand at his command ready to let themselves be sacrificed for a matter of no concern to them.[7] The difference between the savages of Europe and those of America lies chiefly in this, that, while many tribes of the latter have been entirely devoured by their enemies, Europeans know a better way of using the vanquished than by eating them; and they prefer to increase through them the number of their subjects, and so the number of instruments at their command for still more widely spread war.

The depravity of human nature shows itself without disguise in the unrestrained relations of nations to each other, while in the law-governed civil state much of this is hidden by the check of government. This being so, it is astonishing that the word "right" has not yet been entirely banished from the politics of war as pedantic, and that no state has yet ventured to publicly advocate this point of view: For Hugo Grotius, Puffendorf, Vattel, and others—Job's comforters, all of them—are always quoted in good faith to justify an attack, although their codes, whether couched in philosophical or diplomatic terms, have not—nor can have —the slightest legal force, because states, as such, are under no common external authority; and there is no instance of a state having ever been moved by argument to desist from its purpose, even when this was backed up by the testimony of such great men. This homage which every state renders —in words at least—to the idea of right proves that, although it may be slumbering, there is, notwithstanding, to be found in man a still higher natural moral capacity by the aid of which he will in time gain the mastery over the evil principle in his nature, the existence of which he is unable to deny. And he hopes the same of others; for otherwise the word "right" would never be uttered by states who wish to wage war, unless to deride it like the Gallic Prince who declared: "The privilege which nature gives the strong is that the weak must obey them."

The method by which states prosecute their rights can never be by process of law—as it is where there is an external tribunal—but only by war. Through this means, however, and its favorable issue, victory, the question of right is never decided. A treaty of peace makes, it may be, an end to the war of the moment, but not to the conditions of war which at any time may afford a new pretext for opening hostilities; and this we cannot exactly condemn as unjust, because under these conditions everyone is his own judge. Notwithstanding, not quite the same rule applies to states according to the law of nations as holds good of individuals in a lawless condition according to the law of nature, namely, "that they ought to advance out of this condition." This is so because, as states, they have already within themselves a legal constitution, and have therefore advanced beyond the stage at which others, in accordance with their ideas of right, can force them to come under a wider legal constitution. Meanwhile, however, reason, from her throne of the supreme lawgiving moral power, absolutely condemns war as a morally lawful proceeding, and makes a state of peace, on the other hand, an immediate duty. Without a compact between the nations, however, this state of peace cannot be established or assured. Hence there must be an alliance of a particular kind which we may call a covenant of peace (*foedus pacificum*), which would differ from a treaty of peace (*pactum pacis*) in this respect, that the latter merely puts an end to one war, while the former would seek to put an end to war forever. This alliance does not aim at the gain of any power whatsoever of the state, but merely at the preservation and security of the freedom of the state for itself and of other allied states at the same time. The latter do not, however, require, for this reason, to submit themselves like individuals in the state of nature to public laws and coercion. The practicability or objective reality of this idea of federation, which is to extend gradually over all states and so lead to perpetual peace, can be shown. For, if Fortune ordains that a powerful and enlightened people should form a republic—which by its very nature is inclined to perpetual peace—this would serve as a center of federal union for other states wishing to join, and thus secure conditions of freedom among the states in accordance with the idea of the law of nations. Gradually, through different unions of this kind, the federation would extend further and further.

It is quite comprehensible that a people should say: "There shall be no war among us, for we shall form ourselves into a state—that is to say, constitute for ourselves a supreme legislative, administrative, and judicial power which will settle our disputes peaceably." But if this state says: "There shall be no war between me and other states, although I recognize no supreme lawgiving power which will secure me my rights and whose rights I will guarantee"; then it is not at all clear upon what grounds I could base my confidence in my right, unless it were the substitute for that compact on which civil society is based—namely, free federation which reason must necessarily connect with the idea of the law of nations, if indeed any meaning is to be left in that concept at all.

There is no intelligible meaning in the idea of the law of nations as giving a right to make war; for that must be a right to decide what is just, not in accordance with universal, external laws limiting the freedom of each individual, but by means of one-sided maxims applied by force. We must then understand by this that men of such ways of thinking are quite justly served when they destroy one another, and thus find perpetual peace in the wide grave which covers all the abominations of acts of violence as well as the authors of such deeds. For states, in their relation to one another, there can be, according to reason, no other way of advancing from that lawless condition which unceasing war implies, than by giving up their savage lawless freedom, just as individual men have done, and yielding to the coercion of public laws. Thus they can form a State of nations (*civitas gentium*), one, too, which will be ever increasing and would finally embrace all the peoples of the earth. States, however, in accordance with their understanding of the law of nations, by no means desire this, and therefore reject in practice what is correct in theory. Hence, instead of the positive idea of a world-republic, if all is not to be lost, only the negative substitute for it, a federation averting war, maintaining its ground, and ever extending over the world, may stop the current of this tendency to war and shrinking from the control of law. But even then there will be a constant danger that this propensity may break out.[8] *"Then war shall be laid aside, and the harsh world soften to peace: the accursed gates of Battle shall be shut with iron bar and clenching bolt; and godless Frenzy shall sit within upon the weapons of savagery—behind her either hand chained in a hundred brazen bonds, shrieks issuing from those ghastly, bloody lips!"* [Virgil]

THIRD DEFINITIVE ARTICLE OF PERPETUAL PEACE

III. *The rights of men, as citizens of the world, shall be limited to the conditions of universal hospitality.*

We are speaking here, as in the previous articles, not of philanthropy, but of right; and in this sphere hospitality signifies the claim of a stranger entering foreign territory to be treated by its owner without hostility. The latter may send him away again if this can be done without causing his death; but, so long as he conducts himself peaceably, he must not be treated as an enemy. It is not a right to be treated as a guest to which the stranger can lay claim—a special friendly compact on his behalf would be required to make him for a given time an actual inmate—but he has a right of visitation. This right to present themselves to society belongs to all mankind in virtue of our common right of possession of the surface of the earth on which, as it is a globe, we cannot be infinitely scattered, and must in the end reconcile ourselves to existence side by side: at the same time, originally no one individual had more right than another to live in any one particular spot. Uninhabitable portions of the surface, ocean and desert, split up the human community, but in such a way that ships and camels—"the ship of the desert"—make it possible for men to come into touch with one another across these unappropriated regions and to take advantage of our common claim to the face of the earth with a view to a possible intercommunication. The inhospitality of the inhabitants of certain sea coasts—as, for example, the coast of Barbary—in plundering ships in neighboring seas or making slaves of shipwrecked mariners; or the behavior of the Arab Bedouins in the deserts, who think that proximity to nomadic tribes constitutes a right to rob, is thus contrary to the law of nature. This right to hospitality, however—that is to say, the privilege of strangers arriving on foreign soil—does not amount to more than what is implied in a permission to make an attempt at intercourse with the original inhabitants. In this way far distant territories may enter into peaceful relations with one another. These relations may at last come under the public control of law, and thus the human race may be brought nearer the realization of a cosmopolitan constitution.

Let us look now, for the sake of comparison, at the inhospitable behavior of the civilized nations, especially the commercial states of our continent. The injustice which they exhibit on visiting foreign lands and races—this being equivalent in their eyes to conquest—is such as to fill us with horror. America, the negro countries, the Spice Islands, the Cape, etc., were, on being discovered, looked upon as countries which belonged to nobody; for the native inhabitants were reckoned as nothing. In Hindustan, under the pretext of intending to establish merely commercial depots, the Europeans introduced foreign troops; and, as a result, the different states of Hindustan were stirred up to far-spreading wars. Oppression of the natives followed, famine, insurrection, perfidy, and all the rest of the litany of evils which can afflict mankind.

China and Japan (Nippon) which had made an attempt at receiving guests of this kind, have now taken a prudent step. Only a single European people, the Dutch, has China given the right of access to her shores (but not of entrance into the country), while Japan has granted both these concessions; but at the same time, they exclude the Dutch who enter, as if they were prisoners, from social intercourse with the inhabitants. The worst, or from the standpoint of ethical judgment the best, of all this is that no satisfaction is derived from all this violence, that all these trading companies stand on the verge of ruin, that the Sugar Islands, that seat of the most horrible and deliberate slavery, yield no real profit, but only have their use indirectly and for no very praiseworthy object—namely, that of furnishing men to be trained as sailors for the men-of-war and thereby contributing to the carrying on of war in Europe. And this has been done by nations who make a great ado about their piety, and who, while they are quite ready to commit injustice, would like, in their orthodoxy, to be considered among the elect.

The intercourse, more or less close, which has been everywhere steadily increasing between the nations of the earth, has now extended so enormously that a violation of right in one part of the world is felt all over it. Hence the idea of a cosmopolitan right is no fantastical, high-flown notion of right, but a complement of the unwritten code of law—constitutional as well as international law—necessary for the public rights of mankind in general and thus for the realization of perpetual peace. For only by endeavoring to fulfill the conditions laid down by this cosmopolitan law can we flatter ourselves that we are gradually approaching that ideal.

FIRST SUPPLEMENT

CONCERNING THE GUARANTEE OF PERPETUAL PEACE

THIS guarantee is given by no less a power than the great artist nature (*natura daedala rerum*) in whose mechanical course is clearly exhibited a predetermined design to make harmony spring from human discord, even against the will of man. Now this design, although called "Fate" when looked upon as the compelling force of a cause the laws of whose operation are unknown to us, is, when considered as the purpose manifested in the course of nature, called "Providence,"[9] as the deep-lying wisdom of a Higher Cause, directing itself towards the ultimate practical end of the human race and predetermining the course of things with a view to its realization. This Providence we do not, it is true, perceive in the cunning contrivances of nature; nor can we even conclude from the fact of their existence that it is there; but, as in every relation between the form of things and their final cause, we can, and must, supply the thought of a Higher Wisdom, in order that we may be able to form an idea of the possible existence of these products after the analogy of human works of art. The representation to ourselves of the relation and agreement of these formations of nature to the moral purpose for which they were made and which reason directly prescribes to us, is an Idea, it is true, which is in theory superfluous; but in practice it is dogmatic, and its objective reality is well established. Thus we see, for example, with regard to the ideal of perpetual peace, that it is our duty to make use of the mechanism of nature for the realization of that end. Moreover, in a case like this where we are interested merely in the theory and not in the religious question, the use of the word "nature" is more appropriate than that of "providence," in view of the limitations of human reason, which, in considering the relation of effects to their causes, must keep within the limits of possible experience. And the term "nature" is also less presumptuous than the other. To speak of a Providence knowable by us would be boldly to put on the wings of Icarus in order to draw near to the mystery of its unfathomable purpose.

Before we determine the surety given by nature more exactly, we must first look at what ultimately makes this guarantee of peace necessary—the circumstances in which nature has carefully placed the actors in her great theatre. In the next place, we shall proceed to consider the manner in which she gives this surety.

The provisions she has made are as follow: (1) she has taken care that men *can* live in all parts of the world;

(2) she has scattered them by means of war in all directions, even into the most inhospitable regions, so that these, too, might be populated; (3) by this very means she has forced them to enter into relations more or less controlled by law. It is surely wonderful that, on the cold wastes round the Arctic Ocean, there is always to be found moss for the reindeer to scrape out from under the snow, the reindeer itself either serving as food or to draw the sledge of the Ostyak or Samoyeds. And salt deserts, which would otherwise be left unutilized, have the camel, which seems as if created for traveling in such lands. This evidence of design in things, however, is still more clear when we come to know that, besides the fur-clad animals of the shores of the Arctic Ocean, there are seals, walruses and whales whose flesh furnishes food and whose oil fire for the dwellers in these regions. But the providential care of nature excites our wonder above all, when we hear of the driftwood which is carried—whence no one knows—to these treeless shores: for without the aid of this material the natives could neither construct their craft, nor weapons, nor huts for shelter. Here, too, they have so much to do, making war against wild animals, that they live at peace with one another. But what drove them originally into these regions was probably nothing but war.

Of animals, used by us as instruments of war, the horse was the first which man learned to tame and domesticate during the period of the peopling of the earth; the elephant belongs to the later period of the luxury of states already established. In the same way, the art of cultivating certain grasses called cereals—no longer known to us in their original form—and also the multiplication and improvement, by transplanting and grafting, of the original kinds of fruit—in Europe, probably only two species, the crab-apple and wild pear—could only originate under the conditions accompanying established states where the rights of property are assured. That is to say, it would be after man, hitherto existing in lawless liberty, had advanced beyond the occupations of a hunter,[10] a fisherman, or a shepherd to the life of a tiller of the soil, when salt and iron were discovered—to become, perhaps, the first articles of commerce between different peoples—and were sought far and near. In this way the peoples would be at first brought into peaceful relation with one another, and so come to an understanding and the enjoyment of friendly intercourse, even with their most distant neighbors.

Now while nature provided that men could live on all parts of the earth, she also at the same time despotically willed that they *should* live everywhere on it, although against their own inclination and even although this imperative did not presuppose an idea of duty which would compel obedience to nature with the force of a moral law. But, to attain this end, she has chosen war. So we see certain peoples, widely separated, whose common descent is made evident by affinity in their languages. Thus, for instance, we find the Samoyeds on the Arctic Ocean, and again a people speaking a similar language on the Altaian Mountains, a thousand miles away, between whom has pressed in a mounted tribe, war-like in character and of Mongolian origin, which has driven one branch of the race far from the other, into the most inhospitable regions where their own inclination would certainly not have carried them.[11] In the same way, through the intrusion of the Gothic and Sarmatian tribes, the Finns in the most northerly regions of Europe, whom we call Laplanders, have been separated by as great a distance from the Hungarians, with whose language their own is allied. And what but war can have brought the Eskimos to the north of America, a race quite distinct from those of that country and probably European adventurers of prehistoric times? And war, too—nature's method of populating the earth—must have driven the Pescherais in South America as far as Patagonia. War itself, however, is in need of no special stimulating cause, but seems engrafted in human nature, and is even regarded as something noble in itself to which man is inspired by the love of glory apart from motives of self-interest. Hence, among the savages of America, as well as those of Europe in the age of chivalry, martial courage is looked upon as of great value in itself, not merely when a war is going on, as is reasonable enough, but in order that there should be war: and thus war is often entered upon merely to exhibit this quality. So that an intrinsic dignity is held to attach to war in itself, and even philosophers eulogize it as an ennobling, refining influence on humanity, unmindful of the Greek proverb, "War is evil, in so far as it makes more bad people than it takes away."

So much, then, of what nature does for her own ends with regard to the human race as members of the animal world. Now comes the question which touches the essential points in this design of a perpetual peace: "What does nature do in this respect with reference to the end which man's own reason sets before him as a duty? and consequently what does she do to further the realization of his moral purpose? How does she guarantee that what man, by the laws of freedom, ought to do and yet fails to do, he will do, without any infringement of his freedom by the compulsion of nature and that, moreover, this shall be done in accordance with the three forms of public right—constitutional or political law, international law, and cosmopolitan law?" When I say of nature that she *wills* that this or that should take place, I do not mean that she imposes upon us the duty to do it—for only the free, unrestrained, practical reason can do that—but that she does it herself, whether we will or not. *"Fates lead the willing, drive the unwilling."* [Seneca]

1. Even if a people were not compelled through internal discord to submit to the restraint of public laws, war would bring this about, working from without. For, according to the contrivance of nature which we have mentioned, every people finds another tribe in its neighborhood, pressing upon it in such a manner that it is compelled to form itself internally into a state to be able to defend itself as a power should. Now the republican constitution is the only one which is perfectly adapted to the rights of man, but it is also the most difficult to establish and still more to maintain. So generally is this recognized that people often say the members of a republican state would require to be angels, because men, with their self-seeking propensities, are not fit for a constitution of so sublime a form. But now nature comes to the aid of the universal, reason-derived will which, much as we honor it, is in practice powerless. And this she does by means of these very self-seeking propensities, so that it only depends—and so much lies within the power of man—on a good organization of the state for their forces to be so pitted against one another, that the one may check the destructive activity of the other or neutralize its effect. And hence, from the standpoint of reason, the result will be the same as if both forces did not exist, and each individual is compelled to be, if not a morally good man, yet at least a good citizen. The problem of the formation of the state, hard as it may sound, is not insoluble, even for a race of devils, granted that they have intelligence. It may be put thus: "Given a multitude of rational beings who, in a body, require general laws for their own preservation, but each of whom, as an individual, is secretly inclined to exempt himself from this restraint: how are we to order their affairs and how establish for them a constitution such that, although their private dispositions may be really antagonistic,

they may yet so act as a check upon one another that, in their public relations, the effect is the same as if they had no such evil sentiments." Such a problem must be capable of solution. For it deals, not with the moral reformation of mankind, but only with the mechanism of nature; and the problem is to learn how this mechanism of nature can be applied to men, in order so to regulate the antagonism of conflicting interests in a people that they may even compel one another to submit to compulsory laws and thus necessarily bring about the state of peace in which laws have force. We can see, in states actually existing, although very imperfectly organized, that, in externals, they already approximate very nearly to what the *idea* of right prescribes, although the principle of morality is certainly not the cause. A good political constitution, however, is not to be expected as a result of progress in morality; but rather, conversely, the good moral condition of a nation is to be looked for as one of the first fruits of such a constitution. Hence the mechanism of nature, working through the self-seeking propensities of man (which of course counteract one another in their external effects), may be used by reason as a means of making way for the realization of her own purpose—the empire of right—and, as far as is in the power of the state, to promote and secure in this way internal as well as external peace. We may say, then, that it is the irresistible will of nature that right shall at last get the supremacy. What one here fails to do will be accomplished in the long run, although perhaps with much inconvenience to us. As Bouterwek says, "If you bend the reed too much it breaks: he who would do too much does nothing."

2. The idea of international law presupposes the separate existence of a number of neighboring and independent states; and, although such a condition of things is in itself already a state of war (if a federative union of these nations

does not prevent the outbreak of hostilities), yet, according to the *idea* of reason, this is better than that all the states should be merged into one under a power which has gained the ascendancy over its neighbors and gradually become a universal monarchy. For the wider the sphere of their jurisdiction, the more laws lose in force; and soulless despotism, when it has choked the seeds of good, at last sinks into anarchy. Nevertheless, it is the desire of every state, or of its ruler, to attain to a permanent condition of peace in this very way—that is to say, by subjecting the whole world as far as possible to its sway. But nature wills it otherwise. She employs two means to separate nations, and prevent them from intermixing—namely, the differences of language and of religion.[12] These differences bring with them a tendency to mutual hatred, and furnish pretexts for waging war. But, none the less, with the growth of culture and the gradual advance of men to greater unanimity of principle, they lead to concord in a state of peace which, unlike the despotism we have spoken of (the churchyard of freedom), does not arise from the weakening of all forces, but is brought into being and secured through the equilibrium of these forces in their most active rivalry.

3. As nature wisely separates nations which the will of each state, sanctioned even by the principles of international law, would gladly unite under its own sway by stratagem or force; in the same way, on the other hand, she unites nations whom the principle of a cosmopolitan right would not have secured against violence and war. And this union she brings about through an appeal to their mutual interests. The commercial spirit cannot co-exist with war, and sooner or later it takes possession of every nation. For, of all the forces which lie at the command of a state, the power of money is probably the most reliable. Hence states find themselves compelled—not, it is true, exactly from motives of morality—

to further the noble end of peace and to avert war, by means of mediation, wherever it threatens to break out, just as if they had made a permanent league for this purpose. For great alliances with a view to war can, from the nature of things, only very rarely occur, and still more seldom succeed.

In this way nature guarantees the coming of perpetual peace, through the natural course of human propensities: not indeed with sufficient certainty to enable us to prophesy the future of this ideal theoretically, but yet clearly enough for practical purposes. And thus this guarantee of nature makes it a duty that we should labor for this end—an end which is no mere chimera.

SECOND SUPPLEMENT

A Secret Article for Perpetual Peace

A secret article in negotiations concerning public right is, when looked at objectively or with regard to the meaning of the term, a contradiction. When we view it, however, from the subjective standpoint, with regard to the character and condition of the person who dictates it, we see that it might quite well involve some private consideration, so that he would regard it as hazardous to his dignity to acknowledge such an article as originating from him.

The only article of this kind is contained in the following proposition: "The maxims of philosophers, with regard to the conditions of the possibility of a public peace, shall be taken into consideration by states armed for war."

It seems, however, to be derogatory to the dignity of the legislative authority of a state—to which we must, of course, attribute all wisdom—to ask advice from subjects (among whom stand philosophers) about the rules of its behavior to other states. At the same time, it is very advisable that this should be done. Hence the state will silently invite suggestion for this purpose, while at the same time keeping the fact secret. This amounts to saying that the state will allow philosophers to discuss freely and publicly the universal principles governing the conduct of war and establishment of peace; for they will do this of their own accord, if no prohibition is laid upon them. The arrangement between states, on this point, does not require that a special agreement should be made, merely for this purpose; for it is already involved in the obligation imposed by the universal reason of man which gives the moral law. We would not be understood to say that the state must give a preference to the principles of the philosopher rather than to the opinions of the jurist—the representative of state authority —but only that he should be heard. The latter, who has chosen for a symbol the scales of right and the sword of justice, generally uses that sword not merely to keep off all outside influences from the scales; for, when one pan of the balance will not go down, he throws his sword into it; and then *vae victis!* The jurist, not being a moral philosopher, is under the greatest temptation to do this, because it is his business only to apply existing laws and not to investigate whether these are not themselves in need of improvement; and this actually lower function of his profession he looks upon as the nobler, because it is linked to power (as is the case also in both the other faculties, theology and medicine). Philosophy occupies a very low position compared with this combined power. So that it is said, for example, that she is the handmaid of theology; and the same has been said of her position with regard to law and medicine. It is not quite clear, however, "whether she bears the torch before these gracious ladies, or carries the train."

That kings should philosophize, or philosophers become kings, is not to be expected. But neither is it to be desired; for the possession of power is inevitably fatal to the free exercise of reason. But it is absolutely indispensable, for their enlightenment as to the full significance of their vocations, that both kings and sovereign nations, which rule themselves in accordance with laws of equality, should not allow the class of philosophers to disappear, nor forbid the expression of their opinions, but should allow them to speak openly. And since this class of men, by their very nature, are incapable of instigating rebellion or forming unions for purposes of political agitation, they should not be suspected of propagandism.

APPENDIX I

ON THE DISAGREEMENT BETWEEN MORALS AND POLITICS WITH REFERENCE TO PERPETUAL PEACE

IN AN objective sense, morals is a practical science, as the sum of laws exacting unconditional obedience, in accordance with which we *ought* to act. Now, once we have admitted the authority of this idea of duty, it is evidently inconsistent that we should think of saying that we *cannot* act thus. For, in this case, the idea of duty falls to the ground of itself—"*ultra posse nemo obligatur.*" Hence there can be no quarrel between politics, as the practical science of right, and morals, which is also a science of right, but theoretical. That is, theory cannot come into conflict with practice. For, in that case, we would need to understand under the term "ethics" or "morals" a universal doctrine of expediency, or, in other words, a theory of precepts which may guide us in choosing the best means for attaining ends calculated for our advantage. This is to deny that a science of morals exists.

Politics says, "Be wise as serpents"; morals adds the limiting condition, "and guileless as doves." If these precepts cannot stand together in one command, then there is a real quarrel between politics and morals. But if they can be completely brought into accord, then the idea of any antagonism between them is absurd, and the question of how best to make a compromise between the two points of view ceases to be even raised. Although the saying, "Honesty is the best policy," expresses a theory which, alas, is often contradicted in practice, yet the likewise theoretical

31

maxim, "Honesty is better than any policy," is exalted high above every possible objection, is indeed the necessary condition of all politics.

The Terminus of morals does not yield to Jupiter, the Terminus of force; for the latter remains beneath the sway of Fate. In other words, reason is not sufficiently enlightened to survey the series of predetermining causes which would make it possible for us to predict with certainty the good or bad results of human action, as they follow from the mechanical laws of nature; although we may hope that things will turn out as we should desire. But what we have to do, in order to remain in the path of duty guided by the rules of wisdom, reason makes everywhere perfectly clear, and does this for the purpose of furthering her ultimate ends.

The practical man, however, for whom morals is mere theory, even while admitting that what *ought* to be *can* be, bases his dreary verdict against our well-meant hopes really on this: he pretends that he can foresee from his observation of human nature that men will never be willing to do what is required in order to bring about the wished-for results leading to perpetual peace. It is true that the will of all individual men to live under a legal constitution according to the principles of liberty—that is to say, the distributive unity of the wills of all—is not sufficient to attain this end. We must have the collective unity of their united will: all as a body must determine these new conditions. The solution of this difficult problem is required in order that civil society should be a whole. To all this diversity of individual wills there must come a uniting cause in order to produce a common will which no distributive will is able to give. Hence, in the practical realization of that idea, no other beginning of a law-governed society can be counted upon than one that is brought about by force: upon this force, too, public law afterwards rests. This state of things certainly prepares us to meet considerable deviation in actual experience from the theoretical idea of perpetual peace, since we cannot take into account the moral character and disposition of a lawgiver in this connection, or expect that, after he has united a wild multitude into one people, he will leave it to them to bring about a legal constitution by their common will.

It amounts to this. Any ruler who has once got the power in his hands will not let the people dictate laws for him. A state which enjoys an independence of the control of external law will not submit to the judgment of the tribunals of other states when it has to consider how to obtain its rights against them. And even a continent, when it feels its superiority to another, whether this be in its way or not, will not fail to take advantage of an opportunity offered of strengthening its power by the spoliation or even conquest of this territory. Hence all theoretical schemes, connected with constitutional, international, or cosmopolitan law, crumble away into empty impracticable ideals. While, on the other hand, a practical science, based on the empirical principles of human nature, which does not disdain to model its maxims on an observation of actual life, can alone hope to find a sure foundation on which to build up a system of national policy.

Now certainly, if there is neither freedom nor a moral law founded upon it, and every actual or possible event happens in the mere mechanical course of nature, then politics, as the art of making use of this physical necessity in things for the government of men, is the whole of practical wisdom, and the idea of right is an empty concept. If, on the other hand, we find that this idea of right is necessarily to be conjoined with politics and even to be raised to the position of a limiting condition of that science, then the possibility of reconciling them must be admitted. I can thus imagine a moral politician, that is to say, one who understands the principles of statesmanship to be such as do not conflict with morals; but I cannot conceive of a political moralist who fashions for himself such a system of ethics as may serve the interest of statesmen.

The moral politician will always act upon the following principle: "If certain defects which could not have been avoided are found in the political constitution or foreign relations of a state, it is a duty for all, especially for the rulers of the state, to apply their whole energy to correcting them as soon as possible, and to bringing the constitution and political relations on these points into conformity with the Law of Nature, as it is held up as a model before us in the idea of reason; and this they should do even at a sacrifice of their own interest." Now it is contrary to all politics—which is, in this particular, in agreement with morals—to dissever any of the links binding citizens together in the state or nations in the cosmopolitan union, before a better constitution is there to take the place of what has been thus destroyed. And hence it would be absurd indeed to demand that every imperfection in political matters must be violently altered on the spot. But, at the same time, it may be required of a ruler at least that he should earnestly keep the maxim in mind which points to the necessity of such a change, so that he may go on constantly approaching the end to be realized, namely, the best possible constitution according to the laws of right. Even although it is still under despotic rule, in accordance with its constitution as then existing, a state may govern itself on republican lines, until the people gradually become capable of being influenced by the mere idea of the authority of law, just as if it had physical power. And they become accordingly capable of self-legislation, their faculty for which is founded on original right. But if, through the violence of revolution, the product of a bad government, a constitution more in accord with the spirit of law were attained even by unlawful means, it should no longer be held justifiable to bring the people back to the old constitution, although, while the revolution was going on, everyone who took part in it by use of force or stratagem, may have been justly punished as a rebel. As regards the external relations of nations, a state cannot be asked to give up its constitution, even although that be a despotism (which is, at the same time, the strongest constitution where foreign enemies are concerned), so long as it runs the risk of being immediately swallowed up by other states. Hence, when such a proposal is made, the state whose constitution is in question must at least be allowed to defer acting upon it until a more convenient time.[13]

It is always possible that moralists who rule despotically, and are at a loss in practical matters, will come into collision with the rules of political wisdom in many ways, by adopting measures without sufficient deliberation which show themselves afterwards to have been overestimated. When they thus offend against nature, experience must gradually lead them into a better track. But, instead of this being the case, politicians who are fond of moralizing do all they can to make moral improvement impossible and to perpetuate violations of law, by extenuating political principles which are antagonistic to the idea of right, on the pretext that human nature is not capable of good, in the sense of the ideal which reason prescribes.

These politicians, instead of adopting an open, straightforward way of doing things (as they boast), mix themselves up in intrigue. They get at the authorities in power and say what will please them; their sole bent is to sacrifice the nation, or even, if they can, the whole world, with the one end in view that their own private interest may be forwarded. This is the manner of regular jurists (I mean the journeyman lawyer, not the legislator), when they aspire to politics. For, as it is not their business to reason too nicely over legislation, but only to enforce the laws of the country, every legal constitution in its existing form and, when this is changed by the proper authorities, the one which takes its place, will always seem to them the best possible. And the consequence is that everything is purely mechanical. But this adroitness in suiting themselves to any circumstances may lead them to the delusion that they are also capable of giving an opinion about the principles of political constitutions in general, in so far as they conform to ideas of right, and are therefore not empirical, but *a priori*. And they may therefore brag about their knowledge of men—which indeed one expects to find, since they have to deal with so many—without really knowing the nature of man and what can be made of it, to gain which knowledge a higher standpoint of anthropological observation than theirs is required. Filled with ideas of this kind, if they trespass outside their own sphere on the boundaries of political and international law, looked upon as ideals which reason holds before us, they can do so only in the spirit of chicanery. For they will follow their usual method of making everything conform mechanically to compulsory laws despotically made and enforced, even here, where the ideas of reason recognize the validity of a legal compulsory force, only when it is in accordance with the principles of freedom through which a permanently valid constitution becomes first of all possible. The would-be practical man, leaving out of account this idea of reason, thinks that he can solve this problem empirically by looking to the way in which those constitutions which have best survived the test of time were established, even although the spirit of these may have been generally contrary to the idea of right. The principles which he makes use of here, although indeed he does not make them public, amount pretty much to the following sophistical maxims.

1. *Fac et excusa.* Seize the most favorable opportunity for arbitrary usurpation—either of the authority of the state over its own people or over a neighboring people; the justification of the act and extenuation of the use of force will come much more easily and gracefully when the deed is done, than if one has to think out convincing reasons for taking this step and first hear through all the objections which can be made against it. This is especially true in the first case mentioned, where the supreme power in the state also controls the legislature which we must obey without any reasoning about it. Besides, this show of audacity in a statesman even lends him a certain semblance of inward conviction of the justice of his action; and once he has got so far, the god of success (*bonus eventus*) is his best advocate.

2. *Si fecisti, nega.* As for any crime you have committed, such as has, for instance, brought your people to despair and thence to insurrection, deny that it has happened owing to any fault of yours. Say rather that it is all caused by the insubordination of your subjects, or, in the case of your having usurped a neighboring state, that human nature is to blame; for if a man is not ready to use force and steal a march upon his neighbor, he may certainly count on the latter forestalling him and taking him prisoner.

3. *Divide et impera.* That is to say, if there are certain privileged persons, holding authority among the people, who have merely chosen you for their sovereign as *primus inter pares,* bring about a quarrel among them, and make mischief between them and the people. Now back up the people with a dazzling promise of greater freedom; every-

thing will now depend unconditionally on your will. Or
again, if there is a difficulty with foreign states, then to stir
up dissension among them is a pretty sure means of subjecting first one and then the other to your sway, under
the pretext of aiding the weaker.

It is true that nowadays nobody is taken in by these
political maxims, for they are all familiar to everyone.
Moreover, there is no need of being ashamed of them, as
if their injustice were too patent. For the great Powers
never feel shame before the judgment of the common herd,
but only before one another, so that, as far as this matter
goes, it is not the revelation of these guiding principles of
policy that can make rulers ashamed, but only the unsuc-
cessful use of them. For as to the morality of these maxims,
politicians are all agreed. Hence there is always left political prestige on which they can safely count; and this means
the glory of increasing their power by any means that
offer.[14]

In all these twistings and turnings of an immoral doctrine of expediency which aims at substituting a state of
peace for the warlike conditions in which men are placed
by nature, so much at least is clear: that men cannot get
away from the idea of right in their private any more than
in their public relations; and that they do not dare (this
is indeed most strikingly seen in the concept of an international law) to base politics merely on the manipulations
of expediency and therefore to refuse all obedience to the
idea of a public right. On the contrary, they pay all fitting
honor to the idea of right in itself, even although they
should, at the same time, devise a hundred subterfuges and
excuses to avoid it in practice, and should regard force,
backed up by cunning, as having the authority which
comes from being the source and unifying principle of all

right. It will be well to put an end to this sophistry, if not
to the injustice it extenuates, and to bring the false advo-
cates of the mighty of the earth to confess that it is not
right but might in whose interest they speak, and that it is
the worship of might from which they take their cue, as
if in this matter they had a right to command. In order
to do this, we must first expose the delusion by which they
deceive themselves and others; then discover the ultimate
principle from which their plans for a perpetual peace
proceed; and thence show that all the evil which stands
in the way of the realization of that ideal springs from the
fact that the political moralist begins where the moral
politician rightly ends and that, by subordinating principles to an end or putting the cart before the horse, he
defeats his intention of bringing politics into harmony with
morals.

In order to make practical philosophy consistent with
itself, we must first decide the following question: In deal-
ing with the problems of practical reason must we begin
from its material principle—the end as the object of free
choice—or from its formal principle which is based merely
on freedom in its external relation?—from which comes the
following law: *Act so that thou canst will that thy maxim
should be a universal law, be the end of thy action what it
will.*

Without doubt, the latter determining principle of action must stand first; for, as a principle of right, it carries
unconditional necessity with it, whereas the former is ob-
ligatory only if we assume the empirical conditions of the
end set before us—that is to say, that it is an end capable
of being practically realized. And if this end—as, for example, the end of perpetual peace—should be also a duty,
this same duty must necessarily have been deduced from
the formal principle governing the maxims which guide

external action. Now the first principle is the principle of the political moralist; the problems of constitutional, international, and cosmopolitan law are mere technical problems (*problema technicum*). The second or formal principle, on the other hand, as the principle of the moral politician who regards it as a moral problem (*problema morale*), differs widely from the other principle in its methods of bringing about perpetual peace, which we desire not only as a material good, but also as a state of things resulting from our recognition of the precepts of duty.

To solve the first problem—that, namely, of political expediency—much knowledge of nature is required, that her mechanical laws may be employed for the end in view. And yet the result of all knowledge of this kind is uncertain, as far as perpetual peace is concerned. This we find to be so, whichever of the three departments of public law we take. It is uncertain whether a people could be better kept in obedience and at the same time in prosperity by severity or by baits held out to their vanity; whether they would be better governed under the sovereignty of a single individual or by the authority of several acting together; whether the combined authority might be better secured merely, say, by an official nobility or by the power of the people within the state; and, finally, whether such conditions could be long maintained. There are examples to the contrary in history in the case of all forms of government, with the exception of the only true republican constitution, the idea of which can occur only to a moral politician. Still more uncertain is a law of nations, ostensibly established upon statutes devised by ministers; for this amounts in fact to mere empty words, and rests on treaties which, in the very act of ratification, contain a secret reservation of the right to violate them. On the other hand, the solution of the second problem—the problem of political wisdom—forces itself, we may say, upon us; it is quite obvious to everyone, and puts all crooked dealings to shame; it leads, too, straight to the desired end, while, at the same time, discretion warns us not to drag in the conditions of perpetual peace by force, but to take time and approach this ideal gradually as favorable circumstances permit.

This may be expressed in the following maxim: "Seek ye first the kingdom of pure practical reason and its righteousness, and the object of your endeavor, the blessing of perpetual peace, will be added unto you." For the science of morals generally has this peculiarity—and it has it also with regard to the moral principles of public law, and therefore with regard to a science of politics knowable *a priori*—that the less it makes a man's conduct depend on the end he has set before him, his purposed material or moral gain, so much the more, nevertheless, does it conform in general to this end. The reason for this is that it is just the universal will, given *a priori,* which exists in a people or in the relation of different peoples to one another, that alone determines what is lawful among men. This union of individual wills, however, if we proceed consistently in practice, in observance of the mechanical laws of nature, may be at the same time the cause of bringing about the result intended and practically realizing the idea of right. Hence it is, for example, a principle of moral politics that a people should unite into a state according to the only valid concepts of right—the ideas of freedom and equality; and this principle is not based on expediency but upon duty. Political moralists, however, do not deserve a hearing, much and sophistically as they may reason about the existence, in a multitude of men forming a society, of certain natural tendencies which would weaken those principles and defeat their intention. They may endeavor to prove their assertion by giving instances of badly organized constitutions, chosen both from ancient and modern times (as, for example, democracies without a representative system); but such arguments are to be treated with contempt, all the more because a pernicious theory of this kind may perhaps even bring about the evil which it prophesies. For, in accordance with such reasoning, man is thrown into a class with all other living machines which only require the consciousness that they are not free creatures to make them in their own judgment the most miserable of all beings.

Fiat justitia, pereat mundus. This saying has become proverbial, and, although it savors a little of boastfulness, is also true. We may translate it thus: "Let justice rule on earth, although all the rogues in the world should go to the bottom." It is a good, honest principle of right cutting off all the crooked ways made by knavery or violence. It must not, however, be misunderstood as allowing anyone to exercise his own rights with the utmost severity—a course in contradiction to our moral duty; but we must take it to signify an obligation, binding upon rulers, to refrain from refusing to yield anyone his rights or from curtailing them, out of personal feeling or sympathy for others. For this end, in particular, we require, firstly, that a state should have an internal political constitution, established according to the pure principles of right; secondly, that a union should be formed between this state and neighboring or distant nations for a legal settlement of their differences, after the analogy of the universal state. This proposition means nothing more than this: Political maxims must not start from the idea of a prosperity and happiness which are to be expected from observance of such precepts in every state, that is, not from the end which each nation makes the object of its will as the highest empirical principle of political wisdom; but they must set out from the pure concept of the duty of right, from the *"ought"* whose principle is given *a priori* through pure reason. This is the law, whatever the material consequences may be. The world will certainly not perish by any means because the number of wicked people in it is becoming fewer. The morally bad has one peculiarity, inseparable from its nature—in its purposes, especially in relation to other evil influences, it is in contradiction with itself, and counteracts its own natural effect, and thus makes room for the moral principle of good, although advance in this direction may be slow.

Hence objectively, in theory, there is no quarrel between morals and politics. But subjectively, in the self-seeking tendencies of men (which we cannot actually call their morality, as we would a course of action based on maxims of reason) this disagreement in principle exists and may always survive; for it serves as a whetstone to virtue. According to the principle, *Yield not to evils, but go against the stronger* [Virgil], the true courage of virtue in the present case lies not so much in facing the evils and self-sacrifices which must be met here as in firmly confronting the evil principle in our own nature and conquering its wiles. For this is a principle far more dangerous, false, treacherous, and sophistical, which puts forward the weakness in human nature as a justification for every transgression.

In fact the political moralist may say that a ruler and people, or nation and nation, do *one another* no wrong when they enter on a war with violence or cunning, although they do wrong, generally speaking, in refusing to respect the idea of right which alone could establish peace for all time. For, as both are equally wrongly disposed to one another, each transgressing the duty he owes to his neighbor, they are both quite rightly served when they are thus destroyed in war. This mutual destruction stops short at the point of extermination, so that there are always enough of the race left to keep this game going on through all the ages, and a far-off posterity may take warning by them. The Providence that orders the course of the world is hereby justified. For the moral principle in mankind never becomes extinguished, and human reason, fitted for the practical realization of ideas of right according to that principle, grows continually in fitness for that purpose with the ever advancing march of culture; while at the same time, it must be said, the guilt of transgression increases as well. But it seems that, by no theodicy, or vindication of the justice of God, can we justify Creation in putting such a race of corrupt creatures into the world at all, if, that is, we assume that the human race neither will nor can ever be in a happier condition than it is now. This standpoint, however, is too high a one for us to judge from, or to theorize, with the limited concepts we have at our command, about the wisdom of that Supreme Power which is unknowable by us. We are inevitably driven to such despairing conclusions as these if we do not admit that the pure principles of right have objective reality—that is to say, are capable of being practically realized—and, consequently, that action must be taken on the part of the people of a state and, further, by states in relation to one another, whatever arguments empirical politics may bring forward against this course. Politics in the real sense cannot take a step forward without first paying homage to the principles of morals. And, although politics, *per se,* is a difficult art, in its union with morals no art is required; for in the case of a conflict arising between the two sciences, the moralist can cut asunder the knot which politics is unable to untie. Right must be held sacred by man, however great the cost and sacrifice to the ruling power. Here is no half-and-half course. We cannot devise a happy medium between right and expediency—a right pragmatically conditioned. But all politics must bend the knee to the principle of right, and may, in that way, hope to reach, although slowly perhaps, a level whence it may shine upon men for all time.

APPENDIX II

CONCERNING THE HARMONY OF POLITICS WITH MORALS ACCORDING TO THE TRANSCENDENTAL IDEA OF PUBLIC RIGHT

IF I look at public right from the point of view of most professors of law, and abstract from its *matter* or its empirical elements, varying according to the circumstances given in our experience of individuals in a state or of states among themselves, then there remains the *form* of publicity. The possibility of this publicity, every legal title implies. For without it there could be no justice, which can only be thought as before the eyes of men; and without justice there would be no right, for from justice only, right can come.

This characteristic of publicity must belong to every legal title. Hence, as, in any particular case that occurs, there is no difficulty in deciding whether this essential attribute is present or not (whether, that is, it is reconcilable with the principles of the agent or not), it furnishes an easily applied criterion which is to be found *a priori* in the reason, so that in the particular case we can at once recognize the falsity or illegality of a proposed claim (*prae-*

tensio juris), as it were by an experiment of pure reason.

Having thus, as it were, abstracted from all the empirical elements contained in the concept of a political and international law, such as, for instance, the evil tendency in human nature which makes compulsion necessary, we may give the following proposition as the *transcendental formula* of public right: "All actions relating to the rights of other men are wrong if the maxims from which they follow are inconsistent with publicity."

This principle must be regarded not merely as ethical, as belonging to the doctrine of virtue, but also as juridical, referring to the rights of men. For there is something wrong in a maxim of conduct which I cannot divulge without at once defeating my purpose—a maxim which must therefore be kept secret if it is to succeed, and which I could not publicly acknowledge without infallibly stirring up the opposition of everyone. This necessary and universal resistance with which everyone meets me, a resistance therefore evident *a priori,* can be due to no other cause than the injustice with which such a maxim threatens everyone. Further, this testing principle is merely negative; that is, it serves only as a means by which we may know when an action is unjust to others. Like axioms, it has a certainty incapable of demonstration; it is besides easy of application, as appears from the following examples of public right.

1. *Constitutional Law.* Let us take in the first place the public law of the state (*jus civitatis*), particularly in its application to matters within the state. Here a question arises which many think difficult to answer, but which the transcendental principle of publicity solves quite readily: "Is revolution a legitimate means for a people to adopt for the purpose of throwing off the oppressive yoke of a so-called tyrant (*non titulo, sed exercitio talis*)?" The

rights of a nation are violated in a government of this kind, and no wrong is done to the tyrant in dethroning him. Of this there is no doubt. None the less, it is in the highest degree wrong of the subjects to prosecute their rights in this way; and they would be just as little justified in complaining, if they happened to be defeated in their attempt and had to endure the severest punishment in consequence.

A great many reasons for and against both sides of this question may be given if we seek to settle it by a dogmatic deduction of the principles of right. But the transcendental principle of the publicity of public right can spare itself this diffuse argumentation. For, according to that principle, the people would ask themselves, before the civil contract was made, whether they could venture to publish maxims, proposing insurrection when a favorable opportunity should present itself. It is quite clear that if, when a constitution is established, it were made a condition that force may be exercised against the sovereign under certain circumstances, the people would be obliged to claim a lawful authority higher than his. But in that case, the so-called sovereign would be no longer sovereign: or, if both powers—that of the sovereign and that of the people—were made a condition of the constitution of the state, then its establishment (which was the aim of the people) would be impossible. The wrongfulness of revolution is quite obvious from the fact that openly to acknowledge maxims which justify this step would make attainment of the end at which they aim impossible. We are obliged to keep them secret. But this secrecy would not be necessary on the part of the head of the state. He may say quite plainly that the ringleaders of every rebellion will be punished by death, even although they may hold that it was he who first transgressed the fundamental law. For, if a ruler is conscious of possessing irresistible sovereign power (and this must be assumed in every civil constitution, because a sovereign who has not power to protect any individual member of the nation against his neighbor has also not the right to exercise authority over him), then he need have no fear that making known the maxims which guide him will cause the defeat of his plans. And it is quite consistent with this view to hold that, if the people are successful in their insurrection, the sovereign must return to the rank of a subject, and refrain from inciting rebellion with a view to regaining his lost sovereignty. At the same time, he need have no fear of being called to account for his former administration.

2. *International Law.* There can be no question of an international law, except on the assumption of some kind of a law-governed state of things—the external condition under which any right can belong to man. For the very idea of international law, as public right, implies the publication of a universal will determining the rights and property of each individual nation; and this *status juridicus* must spring out of a contract of some sort which may not, like the contract to which the state owes its origin, be founded upon compulsory laws, but may be, at the most, the agreement of a permanent free association such as the federation of the different states, to which we have alluded above. For, without the control of law to some extent, to serve as an active bond of union among different merely natural or moral individuals—that is to say, in a state of nature—there can only be private law. And here we find a disagreement between morals, regarded as the science of right, and politics. The criterion, obtained by observing the effect of publicity on maxims, is just as easily applied, but only when we understand that this agreement binds the contracting states solely with the object that peace may be preserved among them, and between them and other states; in no sense with a view to the acquisition of new territory or

power. The following instances of antinomy occur between politics and morals, which are given here with the solution in each case.

a. "When either of these states has promised something to another (as, for instance, assistance, or a relinquishment of certain territory, or subsidies and such like), the question may arise whether, in a case where the safety of the state thus bound depends on its evading the fulfilment of this promise, it can do so by maintaining a right to be regarded as a double person: firstly, as sovereign and accountable to no one in the state of which that sovereign power is head; and, secondly, merely as the highest official in the service of that state, who is obliged to answer to the state for every action. And the result of this is that the state is acquitted in its second capacity of any obligation to which it has committed itself in the first." But, if a nation or its sovereign proclaimed these maxims, the natural consequence would be that every other would flee from it, or unite with other states to oppose such pretensions. And this is a proof that politics, with all its cunning, defeats its own ends if the test of making principles of action public, which we have indicated, be applied. Hence the maxim we have quoted must be wrong.

b. "If a state which has increased its power to a formidable extent (*potentia tremenda*) excites anxiety in its neighbors, is it right to assume that, since it has the means, it will also have the will to oppress others; and does that give less powerful states a right to unite and attack the greater nation without any definite cause of offense?" A state which would here answer openly in the affirmative would only bring the evil about more surely and speedily. For the greater power would forestall those smaller nations, and their union would be but a weak reed of defense against a state which knew how to apply the maxim *divide et impera.*

This maxim of political expediency then, when openly acknowledged, necessarily defeats the end at which it aims, and is therefore wrong.

c. "If a smaller state by its geographical position breaks up the territory of a greater, so as to prevent a unity necessary to the preservation of that state, is the latter not justified in subjugating its less powerful neighbor and uniting the territory in question with its own?" We can easily see that the greater state dare not publish such a maxim beforehand, for either all smaller states would without loss of time unite against it, or other powers would contend for this booty. Hence the impracticability of such a maxim becomes evident under the light of publicity. And this is a sign that it is wrong, and that, perhaps, in a very great degree; for, although the victim of an act of injustice may be of small account, that does not prevent the injustice done from being very great.

3. *Cosmopolitan Law*. We may pass over this department of right in silence, for, owing to its analogy with international law, its maxims are easily specified and estimated.

In this principle of the incompatibility of the maxims of international law with their publicity, we have a good indication of the non-agreement between politics and morals, regarded as a science of right. Now we require to know under what conditions these maxims do agree with the law of nations. For we cannot conclude that the converse holds, and that all maxims which can bear publicity are therefore just. For anyone who has a decided supremacy has no need to make any secret about his maxims. The condition of a law of nations being possible at all is that, in the first place, there should be a law-governed state of things. If this is not so, there can be no public right, and all right which we can think of outside the law-governed state—that is to say, in the state of nature—is mere private right. Now we have seen above that something of the nature of a federation between nations, for the sole purpose of doing away with war, is the only rightful condition of things reconcilable with their individual freedom. Hence the agreement of politics and morals is only possible in a federative union, a union which is necessarily given *a priori,* according to the principles of right. And the lawful basis of all politics can only be the establishment of this union in its widest possible extent. Apart from this end, all political sophistry is folly and veiled injustice. Now this sham politics has a casuistry, not to be excelled in the best Jesuit school. It has its mental reservation (*reservatio mentalis*): as in the drawing up of a public treaty in such terms as we can, if we will, interpret when occasion serves to our advantage; for example, the distinction between the *status quo* in fact (*de fait*) and in right (*de droit*). Secondly, it has its probabilism; when it pretends to discover evil intentions in another, or makes the probability of their possible future ascendancy a lawful reason for bringing about the destruction of other peaceful states. Finally, it has its philosophical sin (*peccatum philosophicum, peccatillum, bagatelle*) which is that of holding it a trifle easily pardoned that a smaller state should be swallowed up if this be to the gain of a nation much more powerful, pretending that such an increase in power will serve the greater prosperity of the whole world.

Duplicity gives politics the advantage of using one branch or the other of morals, just as suits its own ends. The love of our fellow men is a duty; so, too, is respect for their rights. But the former is only conditional: the latter, on the other hand, an unconditional, absolutely imperative duty; and anyone who would give himself up to the sweet consciousness of well-doing must be first perfectly assured that he has not transgressed its commands. Politics has no difficulty in agreeing with morals in the first sense of the term, as ethics, to secure that men should give to superiors their rights. But when it comes to morals, in its second aspect, as the science of right before which politics must bow the knee, the politician finds it prudent to have nothing to do with compacts and rather to deny all reality to morals in this sense, and reduce all duty to mere benevolence. Philosophy could easily frustrate the artifices of a politics like this, which shuns the light of criticism, by publishing its maxims, if only statesmen would have the courage to grant philosophers the right to ventilate their opinions.

With this end in view, I propose another principle of public right, which is at once transcendental and affirmative. Its formula would be as follows: *All maxims which require publicity in order that they may not fail to attain their end are in agreement both with right and politics.*

For, if these maxims can only attain the end at which they aim by being published, they must be in harmony with the universal end of mankind, which is happiness; and to be in sympathy with this (to make the people contented with their lot) is the real business of politics. Now, if this end should be attainable only by publicity or, in other words, through the removal of all distrust of the maxims of politics, these must be in harmony with the right of the people; for a union of the ends of all is only possible in a harmony with this right.

I must postpone the further development and discussion of this principle till another opportunity. That it is a transcendental formula is quite evident from the fact that all the empirical conditions of a doctrine of happiness, or the *matter* of law, are absent, and that it has regard only to the *form* of universal conformity to law.

If it is our duty to realize a state of public right, if at the same time there are good grounds for hope that this ideal may be realized, although only by an approximation advancing *ad infinitum,* then perpetual peace, following hitherto falsely so-called conclusions of peace which have been in reality mere cessations of hostilities, is no mere empty idea. But rather we have here a problem which gradually works out its own solution and, as the periods in which a given advance takes place towards the realization of the ideal of perpetual peace will, we hope, become with the passing of time shorter and shorter, we must approach ever nearer to this goal.

NOTES

1. An hereditary kingdom is not a state which can be inherited by another state, but one whose sovereign power can be inherited by another physical person. The state then acquires a ruler, not the ruler as such (that is, as one already possessing another realm) the state.

2. It has been hitherto doubted, not without reason, whether there can be laws of permission (*leges permissivae*) of pure reason as well as commands (*leges praeceptivae*) and prohibitions (*leges prohibitivae*). For law in general has a basis of objective practical necessity: permission, on the other hand, is based upon the contingency of certain actions in practice. It follows that a law of permission would enforce what cannot be enforced; and this would involve a contradiction, if the object of the law should be the same in both cases. Here, however, in the present case of a law of permission, the presupposed prohibition is aimed merely at the future manner of acquisition of a right—for example, acquisition through inheritance: the exemption from this prohibition (i.e. the permission) refers to the present state of possession. In the transition from a state of nature to the civil state, this holding of property can continue as a *bona fide*, if usurpatory, ownership, under the new social conditions, in accordance with a permission of the Law of Nature. Ownership of this kind, as soon as its true nature becomes known, is seen to be mere nominal possession (*possessio putativa*) sanctioned by opinion and customs in a natural state of society. After the transition stage is passed, such modes of acquisition are likewise forbidden in the subsequently evolved civil state: and this power to remain in possession would not be admitted if the supposed acquisition had taken place in the civilized community. It would be bound to come

55

to an end as an injury to the right of others, the moment its illegality became patent.

I have wished here only by the way to draw the attention of teachers of the Law of Nature to the idea of a *lex permissiva* which presents itself spontaneously in any system of rational classification. I do so chiefly because use is often made of this concept in civil law with reference to statutes; with this difference, that the law of prohibition stands alone by itself, while permission is not, as it ought to be, introduced into that law as a limiting clause, but is thrown among the exceptions. Thus "this or that is forbidden",—say, Nos. 1, 2, 3, and so on in an infinite progression—while permissions are only added to the law incidentally: they are not reached by the application of some principle, but only by groping about among cases which have actually occurred. Were this not so, qualifications would have had to be brought into the formula of laws of prohibition which would have immediately transformed them into laws of permission. Count von Windischgraetz, a man whose wisdom was equal to his discrimination, urged this very point in the form of a question propounded by him for a prize essay. One must therefore regret that this ingenious problem has been so soon neglected and left unsolved. For the possibility of a formula similar to those of mathematics is the sole real test of a legislation that would be consistent. Without this, the so-called *jus certum* will remain forever a mere pious wish: we can have only general laws valid on the whole; no general laws possessing the universal validity which the concept of law seems to demand.

3. It is usually accepted that a man may not take hostile steps against any one, unless the latter has already injured him by act. This is quite accurate, if both are citizens of a law-governed state. For, in becoming a member of this community, each gives the other the security he demands against injury, by means of the supreme authority exercising control over them both. The individual, however, (or nation) who remains in a mere state of nature deprives me of this security

and does me injury by mere proximity. There is perhaps no active (*facto*) molestation, but there is a state of lawlessness (*status injustus*) which, by its very existence, offers a continual menace to me. I can therefore compel him, either to enter into relations with me under which we are both subject to law, or to withdraw from my neighbourhood. So that the postulate upon which the following articles are based is: "All men who have the power to exert a mutual influence upon one another must be under a civil government of some kind."

A legal constitution is, according to the nature of the individuals who compose the state:

(1) A constitution formed in accordance with the right of citizenship of the individuals who constitute a nation (*jus civitatis*).

(2) A constitution whose principle is international law which determines the relations of states (*jus gentium*).

(3) A constitution formed in accordance with cosmopolitan law, in so far as individuals and states, standing in an external relation of mutual reaction, may be regarded as citizens of one world-state (*jus cosmopoliticum*).

This classification is not an arbitrary one, but is necessary with reference to the idea of perpetual peace. For, if even one of these units of society were in a position physically to influence another, while yet remaining a member of a primitive order of society, then a state of war would be joined with these primitive conditions; and from this it is our present purpose to free ourselves.

4. Lawful, that is to say, external freedom cannot be defined, as it so often is, as the right [*Befugnis*] "to do whatever one likes, so long as this does not wrong anyone else." For what is this right? It is the possibility of actions which do not lead to the injury of others. So the explanation of a "right" would be something like this: "Freedom is the possibility of actions which do not injure anyone. A man does not wrong another— whatever his action—if he does not wrong another": which is empty tautology. My external (lawful) freedom is rather to

be explained in this way: it is the right through which I require not to obey any external laws except those to which I could have given my consent. In exactly the same way, external (legal) equality in a state is that relation of the subjects in consequence of which no individual can legally bind or oblige another to anything, without at the same time submitting himself to the law which ensures that he can, in his turn, be bound and obliged in like manner by this other.

The principle of lawful independence requires no explanation, as it is involved in the general concept of a constitution. The validity of this hereditary and inalienable right, which belongs of necessity to mankind, is affirmed and ennobled by the principle of a lawful relation between man himself and higher beings, if indeed he believes in such beings. This is so, because he thinks of himself, in accordance with these very principles, as a citizen of a transcendental world as well as of the world of sense. For, as far as my freedom goes, I am bound by no obligation even with regard to Divine Laws—which are apprehended by me only through my reason—except in so far as I could have given my assent to them; for it is through the law of freedom of my own reason that I first form for myself a concept of a Divine Will. As for the principle of equality, in so far as it applies to the most sublime being in the universe next to God—a being I might perhaps figure to myself as a mighty emanation of the Divine spirit—there is no reason why, if I perform my duty in the sphere in which I am placed, as that aeon does in his, the duty of obedience alone should fall to my share, the right to command to him. That this principle of equality, (unlike the principle of freedom), does not apply to our relation to God is due to the fact that, to this Being alone, the idea of duty does not belong.

As for the right to equality which belongs to all citizens as subjects, the solution of the problem of the admissibility of an hereditary nobility hinges on the following question: "Does social rank—acknowledged by the state to be higher in the case of one subject than another—stand above desert, or does merit take precedence of social standing?" Now it is obvious that, if high position is combined with good family, it is quite uncertain whether merit, that is to say, skill and fidelity in office, will follow as well. This amounts to granting the favored individual a commanding position without any question of desert; and to that, the universal will of the people—expressed in an original contract which is the fundamental principle of all right—would never consent. For it does not follow that a nobleman is a man of noble character. In the case of the official nobility, as one might term the rank of higher magistracy—which one must acquire by merit—the social position is not attached like property to the person but to his office, and equality is not thereby disturbed; for, if a man gives up office, he lays down with it his official rank and falls back into the rank of his fellows.

5. The lofty appellations which are often given to a ruler—such as the Lord's Anointed, the Administrator of the Divine Will upon earth, and Vicar of God—have been many times censured as flattery gross enough to make one giddy. But it seems to me without cause. Far from making a prince arrogant, names like these must rather make him humble at heart, if he has any intelligence—which we take for granted he has—and reflects that he has undertaken an office which is too great for any human being. For, indeed, it is the holiest which God has on earth—namely, the right of ruling mankind: and he must ever live in fear of injuring this treasure of God in some respect or other.

6. Mallet du Pan boasts in his seemingly brilliant but shallow and superficial language that, after many years experience, he has come at last to be convinced of the truth of the well known saying of Pope: "For Forms of Government let fools contest; Whate'er is best administered is best." If this means that the best administered government is best administered, then, in Swift's phrase, he has cracked a nut to find a worm in it. If it means, however, that the best conducted government is also the best kind of government—that is, the best form of

political constitution—then it is utterly false; for examples of wise administration are no proof of the kind of government. Who ever ruled better than Titus and Marcus Aurelius? And yet the one left Domitian, the other Commodus, as his successor. This could not have happened where the constitution was a good one, for their absolute unfitness for the position was early enough known, and the power of the emperor was sufficiently great to exclude them.

7. A Greek Emperor who magnanimously volunteered to settle by a duel his quarrel with a Bulgarian Prince got the following answer: "A smith who has tongs will not pluck the glowing iron from the fire with his hands."

8. On the conclusion of peace at the end of a war, it might not be unseemly for a nation to appoint a day of humiliation, after the festival of thanksgiving, on which to invoke the mercy of Heaven for the terrible sin which the human race are guilty of, in their continued unwillingness to submit (in their relations with other states) to a law-governed constitution, preferring rather in the pride of their independence to use the barbarous method of war, which after all does not really settle what is wanted—namely, the right of each state in a quarrel. The feasts of thanksgiving during a war for a victorious battle, the hymns which are sung—to use the Jewish expression—"to the Lord of Hosts" are not in less strong contrast to the ethical idea of a father of mankind; for, apart from the indifference these customs show to the way in which nations seek to establish their rights—sad enough as it is—these rejoicings bring in an element of exultation that a great number of lives, or at least the happiness of many, has been destroyed.

9. In the mechanical system of nature to which man belongs as a sentient being, there appears, as the underlying ground of its existence, a certain *form* which we cannot make intelligible to ourselves except by thinking into the physical world the idea of an end preconceived by the Author of the

universe: this predetermination of nature on the part of God we generally call "Divine Providence." In so far as this providence appears in the origin of the universe, we speak of Providence as founder of the world. (*"Providence is a founder; once she orders, they always obey."*—Augustine). As it maintains the course of nature, however, according to universal laws of adaptation to preconceived ends, we call it a ruling providence (*providentia gubernatrix*). Further, we name it the guiding providence (*providentia directrix*), as it appears in the world for special ends, which we could not foresee, but suspect only from the result. Finally, regarding particular events as divine purposes, we speak no longer of providence, but of dispensation (*directio extraordinaria*). As this term, however, really suggests the idea of miracles, although the events are not spoken of by this name, the desire to fathom dispensation, as such, is a foolish presumption in men. For, from one single occurrence, to jump at the conclusion that there is a particular principle of efficient causes and that this event is an end and not merely the natural sequence of a design quite unknown to us is absurd and presumptuous, in however pious and humble a spirit we may speak of it. In the same way to distinguish between a universal and a particular providence when regarding it *materialiter*, in its relation to actual objects in the world (to say, for instance, that there may be, indeed, a providence for the preservation of the different species of creation, but that individuals are left to chance) is false and contradictory. For providence is called universal for the very reason that no single thing may be thought of as shut out from its care. Probably the distinction of two kinds of providence, *formaliter* or subjectively considered, had reference to the manner in which its purposes are fulfilled. So that we have ordinary providence (e.g. the yearly decay and awakening to new life in nature with change of season) and what we may call unusual or special providence (e.g. the bringing of timber by ocean currents to Arctic shores where it does not grow, and where without this aid the inhabitants could not live). Here, although we can

quite well explain the physico-mechanical cause of these phe-
nomena—in this case, for example, the banks of the rivers in
temperate countries are over-grown with trees, some of which
fall into the water and are carried along, probably by
the Gulf Stream—we must not overlook the teleological cause
which points to the providential care of a ruling wisdom above
nature. But the concept, commonly used in the schools of
philosophy, of a cooperation on the part of the Deity or a
concurrence (*concursus*) in the operations going on in the
world of sense must be dropped. For it is, firstly, self-contra-
dictory to couple the like and the unlike together (*gryphes
jungere equis*) and to let Him, who is Himself the entire cause
of the changes in the universe, make good any shortcomings
in His own predetermining providence (which to require this
must be defective) during the course of the world; for example,
to say that the physician has restored the sick with the help
of God—that is to say, He has been present as a support. For
causa solitaria non juvat. God created the physician as well
as his means of healing; and we must ascribe the result wholly
to Him, if we will go back to the supreme First Cause which,
theoretically, is beyond our comprehension. Or we can ascribe
the result entirely to the physician, in so far as we follow up
this event, as explicable in the chain of physical causes, according to the order of nature. Secondly, moreover, such a way
of looking at this question destroys all the fixed principles by
which we judge an effect. But, from the ethico-practical point
of view which looks entirely to the transcendental side of
things, the idea of a divine concurrence is quite proper and
even necessary: for example, in the faith that God will make
good the imperfection of our human justice, if only our feelings
and intentions are sincere; and that He will do this by means
beyond our comprehension, and therefore we should not
slacken our efforts after what is good. Whence it follows, as a
matter of course, that no one must attempt to explain a good
action as a mere event in time by this *concursus;* for that would
be to pretend a theoretical knowledge of the supersensible and
hence be absurd.

10. Of all modes of livelihood the life of the hunter is undoubtedly most incompatible with a civilized condition of society. Because, to live by hunting, families must isolate themselves from their neighbors, soon becoming estranged and spread over widely scattered forests, to be before long on terms of hostility, since each requires a great deal of space to obtain food and raiment.

God's command to Noah not to shed blood (Genesis 9:4-6) is frequently quoted, and was afterwards—in another connection, it is true—made by the baptized Jews a condition to which Christians, newly converted from heathendom, had to conform. *Cf.* Acts 15:20; 21:25. This command seems originally to have been nothing else than a prohibition of the life of the hunter; for here the possibility of eating raw flesh must often occur, and in forbidding the one custom we condemn the other.

11. The question might be put: "If it is nature's will that these Arctic shores should not remain unpopulated, what will become of their inhabitants if, as is to be expected, at some time or other no more driftwood should be brought to them? For we may believe that, with the advance of civilization, the inhabitants of temperate zones will utilize better the wood which grows on the banks of their rivers, and not let it fall into the stream and so be swept away." I answer: the inhabitants of the shores of the River Ob, the Yenisei, the Lena, will supply them with it through trade and take in exchange the animal produce in which the seas of Arctic shores are so rich— that is, if nature has first of all brought about peace among them.

12. Difference of religion! A strange expression, as if one were to speak of different kinds of morality. There may indeed be different historical forms of belief—that is to say, the various means which have been used in the course of time to promote religion—but they are mere subjects of learned investigation, and do not really lie within the sphere of religion. In the same way there are many religious works—the *Zendavesta, Veda,*

Koran, etc.—but there is only one religion, binding for all men and for all times. These books are each no more than the accidental mouthpiece of religion, and may be different according to differences in time and place.

13. These are *permissive* laws of reason which allow us to leave a system of public law, when it is tainted by injustice, to remain just as it is, until everything is entirely revolutionized through an internal development, either spontaneous or fostered and matured by peaceful influences. For any legal constitution whatsoever, even although it conforms only slightly with the spirit of law, is better than none at all—that is to say, anarchy, which is the fate of a precipitate reform. Hence, as things now are, the wise politician will look upon it as his duty to make reforms on the lines marked out by the ideal of public law. He will not use revolutions, when these have been brought about by natural causes, to extenuate still greater oppression than caused them, but will regard them as the voice of nature, calling upon him to make such thorough reforms as will bring about the only lasting constitution—a lawful constitution based on the principles of freedom.

14. It is still sometimes denied that we find, in members of a civilized community, a certain depravity rooted in the nature of man; and it might, indeed, be alleged with some show of truth that not an innate corruptness in human nature, but the barbarism of men, the defect of a not yet sufficiently developed culture, is the cause of the evident antipathy to law which their attitude indicates. In the external relations of states, however, human wickedness shows itself incontestably, without any attempt at concealment. Within the state, it is covered over by the compelling authority of civil laws. For, working against the tendency every citizen has to commit acts of violence against his neighbor, there is the much stronger force of the government which not only gives an appearance of morality to the whole state (*causae non causae*), but, by checking the outbreak of lawless propensities, actually aids

the moral qualities of men considerably, in their development of a direct respect for the law. For every individual thinks that he himself would hold the idea of right sacred and follow faithfully what it prescribes, if only he could expect that everyone else would do the same. This guarantee is in part given to him by the government; and a great advance is made by this step which is not deliberately moral, towards the ideal of fidelity to the concept of duty for its own sake without thought of return. As, however, every man's good opinion of himself presupposes an evil disposition in everyone else, we have an expression of their mutual judgment of one another, namely, that when it comes to hard facts, none of them are worth much; but whence this judgment comes remains unexplained, as we cannot lay the blame on the nature of man, since he is a being in the possession of freedom. The respect for the idea of right, of which it is absolutely impossible for man to divest himself, sanctions in the most solemn manner the theory of our power to conform to its dictates. And hence every man sees himself obliged to act in accordance with what the idea of right prescribes, whether his neighbors fulfil their obligation or not.

COSIMO is an innovative publisher of books and publications that inspire, inform and engage readers worldwide. Our titles are drawn from a range of subjects including health, business, philosophy, history, science and sacred texts. We specialize in using print-on-demand technology (POD), making it possible to publish books for both general and specialized audiences and to keep books in print indefinitely. With POD technology new titles can reach their audiences faster and more efficiently than with traditional publishing.

  ☒ **Permanent Availability:** Our books & publications never go
  out-of-print.

  ☒ **Global Availability:** Our books are always available online at
  popular retailers and can be ordered from your favorite local bookstore.

COSIMO CLASSICS brings to life unique, rare, out-of-print classics representing subjects as diverse as *Alternative Health, Business and Economics, Eastern Philosophy, Personal Growth, Mythology, Philosophy, Sacred Texts, Science, Spirituality* and much more!

COSIMO-on-DEMAND publishes your books, publications and reports. If you are an Author, part of an Organization, or a Benefactor with a publishing project and would like to bring books back into print, publish new books fast and effectively, would like your publications, books, training guides, and conference reports to be made available to your members and wider audiences around the world, we can assist you with your publishing needs.

Visit our website at www.cosimobooks.com to learn more about Cosimo, browse our catalog, take part in surveys or campaigns, and sign-up for our newsletter.

And if you wish please drop us a line at info@cosimobooks.com. We look forward to hearing from you.

CPSIA information can be obtained at www.ICGtesting.com
Printed in the USA
LVOW11s1614071215

465786LV00001B/8/P